HEAD LICE

ELAINE LANDAU

mc Marshall Cavendish
Benchmark
New York

Marshall Cavendish Benchmark
99 White Plains Road
Tarrytown, New York 10591
www.marshallcavendish.us

Expert Reader: Leslie L. Barton, MD, Professor Emerita of Pediatrics,
University of Arizona College of Medicine, Tucson, Arizona

Library of Congress Cataloging-in-Publication Data

Landau, Elaine.
Head lice / by Elaine Landau.
p. cm. — (Head-to-toe health)
Includes bibliographical references and index.
Summary: "Provides basic information about head lice and its prevention"—Provided by publisher.
   ISBN 978-0-7614-3501-3
   1. Pediculosis—Juvenile literature. I. Title.
   RL764.P4L36 2010
   616.5'7205—dc22
   2008016267

Editor: Christine Florie
Publisher: Michelle Bisson
Art Director: Anahid Hamparian
Series Designer: Alex Ferrari

Photo research by Candlepants Incorporated

Cover Photo: Inmagine / Alamy Images

The photographs in this book are used by permission and through the courtesy of:
Art Life Images: Jerome Tisne, 4; Liane Cary, 13; Nils-Johan Norenlind, 15. Photo Researchers Inc.: Sheila Terry, 6;
Eye of Science, 9; Mark Clarke, 18. PhotoTakeUSA.com: Scott Camazine, 11. Alamy Images: Jack Sullivan, 19;
Photo Edit Inc.: Cindy Charles, 23. Getty Images: Denis Felix, 25.

Printed in Malaysia
1 3 5 6 4 2

Contents

AN UNWELCOME GUEST . . . 5

ALL ABOUT HEAD LICE . . . 8

HERE, THERE, AND EVERYWHERE . . . 12

HEAD LICE—PLEASE LEAVE! . . . 17

GONE FOR GOOD? . . . 22

GLOSSARY . . . 27

FIND OUT MORE . . . 28

INDEX . . . 30

An Unwelcome Guest

Your head itches. You've been scratching a lot, but it hasn't helped. You're not the only one, either. Other kids at school are scratching their heads, too. You've seen them in the classroom, in the cafeteria, and on the playground. What's making everyone's head itch?

The answer is soon clear. Some kids at school have head lice. Head lice are tiny insects that can live on a person's head. Your mother checks your head and discovers that you have them, too.

"YUCK!" That's the first word out of your mouth when you hear the news. You don't want those creepy creatures on your head. No one does, yet it happens.

SMALL INSECTS, BIG PROBLEM

Head lice are a growing problem. Hundreds of millions of people get them every year. Each year 6 to 12 million people

◀ **A very itchy head is a tell-tale sign of head lice.**

DID YOU KNOW?

Think getting head lice is a new problem?
That's not the case. Head lice have been around for
thousands of years. That's even older than your parents! The
ancient Greeks and Romans had head lice. Kids back then
were scratching their heads, too.

in the United States are treated for head lice. That's more than all the people living in the country of Greece.

There's even worse news if you're a kid. Most of the people who get head lice are children. Head lice are most common among young people from three to eleven years old.

Yet if you get head lice, there's no need to panic. Unlike body lice, head lice do not carry disease. They may make your head itchy, but they aren't painful. It isn't really that hard to get rid of them, either. If you want to know more about head lice, just keep reading.

ALL ABOUT HEAD LICE

Head lice are small, six-legged creatures. Adult lice may be either pale gray or brown. These insects have flat bodies and nearly oval heads. A fully grown louse (the singular of lice) is only about the size of a sesame seed.

Head lice cannot fly, hop, swim, or jump. They move about by crawling. Each of their legs has a claw that helps them cling to your hair.

Don't let the word "crawl" fool you, though. Head lice are small but speedy. They move at a rate of about 9 inches per minute.

MAKING THEMSELVES AT HOME

Head lice are **parasites**. That means they cannot survive on their own for very long. They need to live off a human **host**. That could be you or another human.

Adult head lice feed every few hours. They take a tiny amount of blood from your scalp. When they feed, they also

A high-powered microscope captures a louse clinging to human hair.

inject a tiny amount of their saliva into your blood.

Their saliva produces an **allergic reaction** in most people. That's what makes you itch. However, the itching doesn't always happen right away. It takes some people a while to react to louse saliva.

Sometimes people have a severe reaction. They develop a red, crusty rash. Other people don't react at all. Yes, you can have head lice and not even itch!

CHICKENS AREN'T THE ONLY ONES LAYING EGGS

Adult head lice are busy **breeders**. A female lives for about three to four weeks. During that time she lays about ten eggs, or **nits**, daily.

NEEDY LITTLE CREATURES

How long do you think head lice can live without a human host?

A. More than two weeks

B. Eight days

C. Up to three days

The correct answer is C. In addition, nits cannot hatch at a temperature lower than that found near a human scalp. That means they can't hatch at room temperature.

These oval-shaped, yellowish white eggs are smaller than adult lice. The nits stick to your hair strands, near your scalp. It's easy to mistake the nits for dandruff. You can't flick them off with your finger, however.

The eggs hatch in ten days to two weeks. The newly hatched head lice, or **nymphs**, grow quickly. In nine to twelve days they are adults.

The adult head lice mate. Then the females begin to lay eggs. If someone with head lice isn't treated, this cycle continues. It will repeat itself about every three weeks.

All this activity takes place on your head. Yet people who have head lice often don't know it right away.

A serious case of head lice can be seen above where many nits are attached to this person's hair.

Here, There, and Everywhere

True or false? Head lice breed in dirty areas. People who do not wash often are more likely to have head lice.

If you think this is true, think again. Head lice don't breed in or feed on dirt. In fact, they prefer clean scalps to dirty ones.

It doesn't matter if you're rich, poor, or somewhere in between. Anyone can get head lice. They can even infest royalty. These insects are just looking for a home.

You also can't get head lice from your dog, cat, or any other pet. It can't happen even if you cuddle your pets or sleep with them. You can only get head lice from another human who already has them.

Head lice prefer clean hair and scalps. Close contact allows lice to travel from one head to another.

SOME TELLING SIGNS

It's not always easy to spot lice and nits in your hair. Yet there are some signs that you may have them. If you are experiencing the things listed below, ask the person taking care of you to check your head for lice.

- A "ticklish" feeling in your hair that feels like something is moving around on your head.
- Lots of itching.
- Sores on your scalp that can be caused by scratching.

KIDS AND HEAD LICE

Why do young people get head lice more often than adults? Head lice are often spread when kids are together at schools, camps, or on the playground. There's lots of chances for head-to-head contact at these kinds of places.

Just think about it. You sit next to other kids in class. What if you've got a secret to tell the kid in the next aisle? As you lean over to whisper it, your head touches that person's head. If that kid has head lice, you may soon be scratching, too.

You're in close contact with kids at play as well. Have you ever played the game called telephone? You sit in a circle and lean over to whisper something to the kid next to you. It's a fun game, and heads often touch while playing it.

Something as common as a whisper between friends gives head lice an opportunity to infect another person.

Did you go to camp last summer? Some camps offer baseball or horseback riding. At times kids forget to bring their own helmets, so they borrow other kids' helmets. If someone has head lice and lends out a helmet, can you guess what can happen?

Have you ever let someone use your comb or brush? Maybe you left your hat or scarf home on a cold winter day. Did you borrow somebody else's to keep warm? These are still other ways to get head lice. As you can see, close contact makes it easy for head lice to travel.

HEAD LICE– PLEASE LEAVE!

Head lice, head lice go away
Don't come back another day.

Head lice are a little like the rain in that children's rhyme. If you have them, you want them to go away. Yet unlike rain, you don't want them to come again another day. You never want them to come back.

There are different treatments available to get rid of head lice. Ignoring them isn't one of them. These insects won't leave on their own. If you want to be rid of head lice, you have to take action.

First, make sure that you really have head lice. Dandruff or other bugs are sometimes mistaken for lice. Don't try to check your own head for lice. You can't do a thorough job on your own.

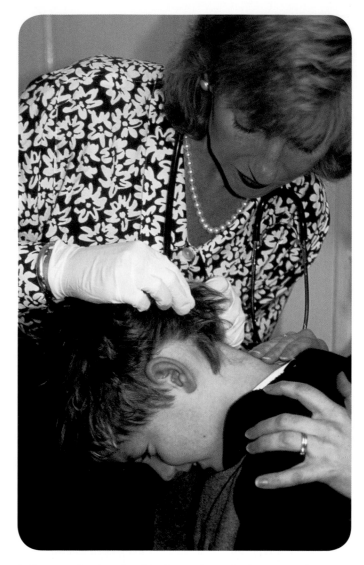
A thorough check of hair and scalp is a good way to detect head lice.

A responsible adult should help you with this. It can be a parent, the school nurse, or someone else who takes care of you.

CHECKING FOR HEAD LICE

Head lice can be spotted without a magnifying glass. However, sometimes a flashlight and a handheld magnifier can be helpful. When checking, it's usually a good idea to part the hair in sections.

It's also important to be thorough. Your head should be

checked from one side to the other. Tiny red bite marks often can be found behind the ears or at the back of the neck.

Don't worry. You won't have millions of lice on your head. Most people have only between ten and twenty live lice, along with some nits.

GETTING RID OF THOSE CREEPY CREATURES

Chemical antilouse shampoos are used to treat head lice. Only a responsible adult should apply these. Some of these treatments need to be used again in seven to ten days. Others do not.

The chemical shampoos kill head lice. However, they do not work on the nits. These must be removed with a fine-tooth comb known as a nit comb.

Hopefully, after you've been treated, the lice will be gone. However, if there are still lice after two weeks, something went wrong.

The best way to remove nits is by using a fine-tooth nit comb.

HOME REMEDIES, BEWARE!

People have tried all sorts of home **remedies** to get rid of head lice. These include covering a person's hair with mayonnaise, butter, cooking oil, or petroleum jelly (Vaseline). The idea here is to smother the lice so they can't breath. It's best to pass on these remedies. Some of the lice might die, but not all of them. These remedies also don't work on nits. Before long the nits will hatch and become adults.

Some people have used gasoline or kerosene to get rid of head lice. Never try this. These products are highly **flammable**. At times children have been badly burned or have even died when they accidentally caught on fire. Gas and kerosene can also be absorbed through the skin. This can be toxic and may cause death.

Some nits might have been left in your hair. You might also still be having head-to-head contact with someone who has live lice.

Sometimes head lice survive a chemical shampoo treatment. In these cases the insects may have become **resistant** to the chemicals used. If this happens, you need to see your doctor or other health-care provider. That person will suggest another treatment. You may also need medical care if there are sores on your scalp. These can develop if you break the skin when you scratch. The sores can become infected. If this happens, you'll need medicine to clear up the infection.

If you have head lice, everyone in your family should be checked for head lice, too. There's lots of chances for head-to-head contact at home. Family members sometimes share clothing, towels, and bed linens. They may hug a lot, too. That's great, but it's even better when everyone in the family is lice-free.

Gone for Good?

Can you get head lice more than once? You bet you can! In fact, many people do. Having had head lice does not give you **immunity** from them in the future.

There is simply no sure way to avoid ever getting head lice. Yet don't feel completely helpless. Following a few easy rules can lessen your chances of hosting these unwanted guests.

KEEPING HEAD LICE FAR AWAY

Start by trying to avoid head-to-head contact at school or play. Let's say that you're invited to a pajama party. Have fun at the party, but don't switch pillows with other kids. If possible, bring your own sleeping bag.

Don't borrow other people's combs, brushes, hair clips, or hair ribbons, either. Remember to take along your own instead. The same goes for using other people's hats, scarves, and helmets.

When in close contact with friends, such as at a pajama party, never share pillows or sleeping bags.

GETTING RID OF HEAD LICE WITHOUT CHEMICALS

Biologists at the University of Utah have come up with a new device called the LouseBuster. It's a little like a hair dryer with a rakelike hand piece at the end of a hose. Warm air flows through the hose. It kills head lice and nits by drying them out. One of the biologists had accidentally stumbled on the idea for the LouseBuster. He had been studying lice that infest birds. Yet when he came to the University of Utah, the lice he was working with died. Utah's air was too dry for them. He wondered if head lice could be dried out, too, and found that they could. The LouseBuster may soon be ready to be sold.

AFTER THOSE CREEPY CREATURES ARE GONE

What if you recently had head lice? There are more steps to take to help make sure they don't come back. Can you remember what you wore on the two days before you were treated for head lice? This clothing should be machine washed in hot water and dried on a high-heat setting. The same should be done with your bed linens. Any items that can't be

To ensure that you've gotten rid of all head lice, be sure to wash your linens in hot water.

machine washed should be dry cleaned. You want to be sure no live lice are left on these items.

The combs or brushes you used should be thoroughly cleaned as well. Washing them with soap and hot water will do the trick. Some people prefer soaking their combs and brushes in a bowl of rubbing alcohol for an hour. Then they rinse them off with water. The carpet and furniture should also be vacuumed. It isn't necessary to spend a lot of time on this. You are not likely to get head lice again through contact with these items. However, it may be helpful to vacuum the places where you usually sit.

Did you hug or sleep with a stuffed animal while you had lice? Don't worry, you don't have to throw it away. Simply keep it in a sealed plastic bag for two weeks. When you take it out, it will be lice free. Hopefully, both of you will stay that way.

No one will ever welcome head lice. Yet if you get them, remember that there's nothing to be ashamed of. It can happen to anyone. The idea is to get rid of them. Once that's done, you can forget that those creepy creatures were ever on your head.

Glossary

allergic reaction — unpleasant reaction caused by the body's sensitivity to a substance

biologist — a scientist who studies plant and animal life

breeder — an insect or animal that mates and has young

flammable — likely to catch on fire

host — an animal or plant that other animals or plants live off of

immunity — protection against a disease or other conditions

nits — the eggs laid by head lice

nymphs — newly hatched head lice

parasite — an insect, plant, or animal that lives off another

remedy — something that solves a problem

resistant — the ability not to be affected by something

FIND OUT MORE

BOOKS

Glaser, Jason. *Head Lice*. Mankato, MN: Capstone Press, 2005.

Llewellyn, Claire. *The Best Book of Bugs*. New York: Kingfisher, 2005.

Murphy, Patricia J. *Investigating Insects with a Scientist*. Berkeley Heights, NJ: Enslow, 2004.

Richardson, Adele. *Insects*. Mankato, MN: Capstone Press, 2005.

Somervill, Barbara A. *Lice: Head Hunters*. New York: PowerKids Press, 2007.

Winner, Cherie. *Everything Bug: What Kids Really Want to Know About Insects and Spiders*. Chanhassen, MN: NorthWord, 2004.

DVDS

Basic Facts About Insects. Educational Video Network, Inc., 2004.

Eyewitness: Insect. Big Kids Productions, Inc., 2006.

WEB SITES

Bug Fun!

www.uky.edu/Ag/Entomology/ythfacts/bugfun/bugfun.htm

Check out this fun Web site to learn all about insects. Be sure to see the links detailing the different insect crafts and projects.

Head Lice Info for Kids

www.headlice.org/kids

See this Web site for lots of great information on head lice. Don't miss the "Head Games" link for some fun word searches and scrambles.

INDEX

Page numbers in **boldface** are illustrations.

allergic reaction, 10, 27

biologist, 24, 27
body, 8, **9**
breeders/breeding, 10–11, 12, 27
brushes, hair, 16

checking for head lice, 18–19
chemical shampoos, 19, 21
clothing, 16
color, 8, **9**
combs, 16
contact, head-to-head, 12, 14–15, 16
contracting lice, 12, 14–15, 16

diagnosing, 18–19

eggs, 10–11, **11**

flammable, 20, 27
food source, 8, 10
frequency of occurrence, 5, 7

hair brushes, 16
hats, 16
head-to-head contact, 12, 14–15, 16
helmets, 16
home remedies, 20
host, 8, 10, 27

immunity, 22, 27
itching, 10

legs, 8, **9**
lice/louse, **9**
life cycle, 10–11
LouseBuster, 24

nit comb, 19, **19**
nits, 10–11, **11**, 27
nymphs, 11, 27

occurrence in the U.S., 5, 7

parasites, 8, 27
prevention, 22, 24, 25–26

remedy, 20, 27
resistant, 21, 27

saliva, 10
scarves, 16
shampoos, 19, 21
symptoms, 5, 14

treatment, 17–21

ABOUT THE AUTHOR

Award-winning author Elaine Landau has written more than three hundred books for young readers. Many of these are on health and science topics. For Marshall Cavendish, Landau has written *Asthma*; *Bites and Stings*; *Broken Bones*; *Bumps, Bruises, and Scrapes*; *Cavities and Toothaches*; and *The Common Cold* for the Head-to-Toe Health series.

Landau received a bachelor's degree in English and journalism from New York University and a master's degree in library and information science from Pratt Institute. You can visit Elaine Landau at her Web site: www.elainelandau.com.